THE SLACKMASTER

The Slackmaster is the working persons survival guide to slacking.

ISBN 978-1-257-95638-8

Disclaimer:

Warning: Slacking is a form of extreme risk taking and can be habit forming. Slacking could be hazardous to your employment status. Slack at your own risk. I am in no way responsible for your actions if you shall choose to become a Slackmaster. You are responsible for your own decisions. So Proceed with caution, if you dare. The contents of these pages are for entertainment purposes only. (Maybe)

Contents

CHAPTER 1:   Intro to Slackmaster, Do You Want To Play The Game?

CHAPTER 2:   Slacking, It's What Makes The World Go Around

CHAPTER 3:   The Slackers' Master Tips

CHAPTER 4:   Workplace Problems a Slackmaster Might Encounter

CHAPTER 5:   Picking Your Opponent Apart

CHAPTER 6:   Defensive Slacking

CHAPTER 7:   Create Your Own Benefits

CHAPTER 8:   Fifty Excuses For Calling In Sick.

CHAPTER 9:   Revenge, A Dish Which Is Best Served Cold

CHAPTER 10:   Team Slack

CHAPTER 11:   Stupidity Should Hurt, Bad!

CHAPTER 12:   Victim Of Your Own Success

CHAPTER 13:   Typical Days Of Slacking

CHAPTER 14:   Hide And Go Sleep

CHAPTER 1:

Intro to Slackmaster, Do You Want To Play The Game?

In this book, you will learn all about the steps of becoming a true Slackmaster at work. This book will teach you the ins and outs and which steps to use and when to apply certain steps in a particular situation. Many of the steps can be applied to just about any job or career that you may have.

First, let's start off by describing the differences between a job and a career. A job may be working at a place in order to pass time. More often than not it's a job that you can pretty much "take it" or "leave it", but at least (in some cases) pays the bills. It may be just until a better job or higher paying job comes along, or perhaps while you are going to school to start a career. Whatever the job may be, it often is one that you don't care about much and is not usually for long term.

However, sometimes a job can end up turning into a career if the right slacking techniques are used. A career on the other hand, is usually long term and not always, but sometimes there is a better chance of actually liking or not minding what you are doing for a living. This is where the job can turn into a career. For example you may not like what you are doing at work but are willing to stick it out because of perhaps a good pension, easy work, or some other reason.

Now, what you've been waiting for. Slackmaster, and what is it? Slackmaster can best be defined as: One who has mastered all the steps in slacking, knowing when, where, and how to outsmart the opponent, by doing the least amount of work possible.

So in other words, all you have to do is just what you have to, and nothing more. Just do the bare minimum all the time. A big step to becoming a Slackmaster is to do something to the least of its difficulty.

Even if that means sitting down to think about something before you do it. Slacking after awhile becomes more like an art form that can be used in any type of job.

Once a master, you'll be able to find a way to just get by, doing less than minimum, and excel at what work you actually happen to do. Just remember that slacking, when used correctly will always be effective until the slacker has no more need for it. Not only is slacking good to do, it also creates job security. Something everyone can use in these tough times.

Now it's time to follow the steps on how to turn a job or career that you hate into a job or career that you essentially like and don't mind doing for a living. You will actually end up having fun along with making fun of the people and the job that you once hated. We will be going thru many different examples of jobs and situations that you encounter. However, most of the steps can be applied towards just about any type of job or career that you may have.

One thing you'll always need to remember is everyone slacks at some point. All of your coworkers, even all the management, administrators, and CEO's slack at some point. Never feel guilty for what you have done or not done for that matter. Guilt has no place in slacking, so get over it. The management and administrators are some of the biggest slackers in the world and have no problems cashing their huge pay checks.

You've all heard the saying "stress kills". It's true and not only that, stress just plan "sucks". Unfortunately, most stress comes from the workplace, so why not relieve stress at work instead of receive it. In addition to relieving stress, slacking is also a great way to keep your mind sharp. It helps you become aware of your surroundings and the way people really operate. Slacking will help you feel people out and know what they are thinking or are going to do next. Slacking is more important than people realize.

CHAPTER 2:

Slacking, It's What Makes The World Go Around

In this next chapter you'll read about the Steps in becoming a Slackmaster. There are many different steps that you need to learn, memorize, implement, and master. The first three steps are not only the hardest but the most important to remember. If you don't achieve the first three steps all the others will be that much harder for you to become skilled at. However, once the first three steps are mastered the rest will fall into place for you.

Step 1: The game, do you want to play?

The first and most important step to remember while working is: Work is nothing more than a Game; a mind game if you will. Work is a big part of the game of life, there just is no way to avoid. Your opponent(s) can be just one person or sometimes many that are connected to your job, such as a boss, management, or even fellow co-workers. Your mind has to be stronger and most importantly, you have to outsmart your opponent(s). And the object of the game is: TO WIN! Well actually, it's to do as little work as humanly possible, and continue to do so as long as you want to. It's all about mind games. So let the games begin.

Step 2: Don't get mad, get even.

The next crucial step to follow is: Don't Get Mad, Get

Even. No matter how much something or someone ticks you

off; never, under any circumstances, let the opponent see that

you are mad or dissatisfied about anything, especially them.

Because getting mad can ultimately result in losing the game.

Remember the three C's and remain Calm, Cool, & Collected.

Even if that means walking away from a particular situation to

"cool off". That will give you the opportunity to collect

yourself. Sometimes you might have to bite your tongue.

When you go home, collect your thoughts and relax, and do

something for yourself for a change. Just remember the next

time you are having a bad day, it will be easier for your

opponent to pick you apart and make your life a living hell.

But we all know, that you'll be able to fire back upon your

opponent and give them the same hell later. This is the whole

point to step two.

Step 3: Don't worry, pretend to be happy.

The third and most important step is: always try to show a "Positive Attitude", even if that means you have to pretend to be happy and always in a good mood. That really irritates people the most. Being positive and happy towards your opponent will always pay off. The happier you are (or pretend to be), the angrier the opponent becomes. That is when you can move right in and pick them apart. We'll discuss this technique in a later chapter. So, remember to always keep grinning, it'll always keep people wondering what you are up to.

There are so many more steps and once you become more involved in slacking you'll be able to add your own steps once your slacking turns into an art form. Here are a few more to help get you started.

Step 4: Mad as hell but fun.

The fourth step to remember is to have fun. It will be a cat and mouse game, that once mastered, you'll actually learn to have fun at work. One day it'll come to you and you'll realize just how much fun it is to chew people up and spit them out, especially when you are the "little guy", "blue collar worker", the one that all upper management looks down upon as low skilled scum and thinks you're nothing but trash. So just keep reading on and you'll be the one looking down upon upper management. It'll be so much fun that you'll have the ability to turn the hair of your opponent(s) grey and in some cases making them quit. Game over, right? Wrong, it'll never be over until you are sitting on your ass collecting a check every month from the very people who were trying to get you to quit by trying to make your life a living hell.

Meanwhile, they'll have to continue to work and slave the rest of their lives. It may sound cruel, but who wants to work up till the day they die?

The only people that work that long are the ones that will someday look back and wish they would have became a "Slackmaster". After all, do you really think that the CEO's, President's, Chief's, Managers, Supervisors, Bosses, and so called fellow co-workers give a crap about you? They are all just pretending. There may be an exception here and there, but most would "Throw you under the bus" in a heartbeat! See step 3.

Step 5: Show and tell.

The fifth step is: Pretending and Acting. This is
where you get to brush up on your acting skills by pretending
that you actually care. You need to act like the job means
something to you by pretending that you are very concerned
about the business or company. A good way to do this is when
you have an opportunity to go to a meeting and are able to
express your (fake) ideas and concerns. As long as it is on
company time, why not; it gives you an excuse to slack and
waste time. What it's really all about is wasting time and
killing 8 hours of each day. Take advantage of any time you
can kill.

Look at how much time is wasted by meetings that
management goes to. They setup the meetings. At these
meetings, they all pull out their "not so smart" phones and look
at their fake schedules and then schedule yet another meeting.

In many cases, half, if not more of their day is wasted sitting in meetings where no one can make a decision on anything. They then schedule another meeting and replay the same scenario. It's a joke! All they are doing is trying to make their job look important and so should you!

Step 6: Busy as hell.

The sixth step is: Always act like you are working. Act like you are trying very hard. Try to always make it appear to management and other co-workers that you are always busy. They can never come back and say that you are lazy and don't try. This is especially important around other co-workers, because one of them may be a "nark" or "teacher's pet" and are there ready to snitch on you. The nosey nark will even be nice to you, but as soon as you turn your back, the brown-noser will run to management to further their own gain. This leads into the next two steps.

Step 7: Taking notes.

Step 7 is also very, very important. Take notes and memos throughout the day (it kills lots of time). This should include what others are or aren't doing. Don't forget to include management and co-workers both. Especially when one of them might be trying to get away with a scam, also known as "Fringe Benefits". Sometimes, it's also referred to as "Creating Your Own Benefits", which we'll talk about in a later chapter. Someday, you might find yourself backed into a corner and might just need to use your notes about someone to help you get out of a situation. Don't forget to include dates and times as well. The more details that you can take in, the better.

Step 8: Never Tell.

The eighth step is one of the most, if not the most important of all steps. In fact it probably shouldn't even be a step, it is just a given. That's why it's step 8, it's common sense, but has to be said anyway. Never, Never, Never tell ANYONE what you are up to or what you are really doing. You cannot trust telling anyone about your newly found hobby of slacking at work. Not even friends. Even if you think someone is your friend, it will ALWAYS come back to haunt you. See Step six. You don't want others to know that you might be slacking. They will try to play the game as well giving you a disadvantage. The deck is always stacked in your favor if no one else knows. It's better to just sit and hide somewhere and watch someone else work instead. But it's a horrible feeling if you are the one doing the work and they are sitting watching you.

Step 9: You can do what?

On to the ninth step: Never, Ever show how much work you are capable of doing. If you go all out and totally "bust your _ss", then you'll always be expected to keep up that pace all the time. This is especially true when you are new. It's hard as a new employee because you want to show that you can do the job and or pass the probationary period. Always keep plenty in reserve; that way you won't have to work so hard. Another thing to remember is that sometimes, but not always, if someone fails in a series of given tasks over an extended period of time, they will then just reassign him or her to another location with the same job.

However, if someone excels at given tasks, they might reassign him or her to another more menial job because he or she is making all the other "slugs" look bad. If this happens, just remember that your pay will not go up either.

You'll be expected to do more work than everyone else for the same pay. This is especially true with Union jobs, but can apply to many others as well.

Step 10: Hit the ground walking.

Step ten is all about starting off slow and working your way up to a full slack mode. If you try to slack too much at once, you'll become overwhelmed and will lose the game for sure. You need to pace yourself and learn the ropes and the do's and don'ts of the Slackmaster. Learn the comings and goings of coworkers and others, learn their habits, how they are getting by, and see how they are slacking and take it to a new level.

There are many more steps that you'll discover along the way, but remember this: Hard work is rewarded with more work!

CHAPTER 3:

The Slackers' Master Tips

Here are some excellent tips on staying ahead of the game. All you really have to do is more work than the laziest person and you'll be fine. It shouldn't be hard to figure out who the lazy person is. Once you have figured out who they are, watch them and observe what and how much work they really do. Then, management won't come back and say that you do the least amount of work around here.

There is a difference between being a slacker and being lazy. People who are lazy couldn't do an honest day's work if their life depended on it. They are even lazy at home in their everyday life. They have no ambition and their brains are just wired that way.

People who are slacking are very capable of working hard and doing an honest day's work. However, they choose not to. That can be for many reasons: under paid, underappreciated, dead end job, no raises, no incentive, low morale, why work when nobody else does, the list just goes on and on.

Don't backstab people or talk about them when they are not around. Remember, word gets around a lot faster than you think, and can backfire on you. Besides, it's a lot more fun to stab people in the face instead of the back. That way it gives them something to really think about. If not, it'll at least "_iss them off". It also helps to be as sarcastic as you can. It's even best to be a "smart_ss" as long as you don't forget to pretend that you are joking around. You know it's true and so do they, because the truth hurts. It helps if you make a joke or a mockery out of a person or situation rather than talking negative. That way people won't think of you as a negative person.

24

Instead, they will think of you as a positive person who is always in a good mood trying to have a good time or making a bad situation better. Only you will know that it's the truth and you really mean it, but your opponent(s) will see it as a joke and they won't know the difference anyway.

When it comes to slacking, it's all about you. Who cares what others think about you. What they think is meaningless. Even if they hate you, it doesn't matter. You are working for yourself not them. If they hate you, sometimes that can work to your advantage. Let them get upset instead. It's ok if you can't stand someone. That just means you don't have to be around them or talk to them, just ignore them instead of hating them. Remember, hating someone does nothing to the person you hate, but hate is an emotional cancer inside of you. It only affects "YOU" both physically and mentally; not them. So just ignore people you dislike, it'll "_iss them off" even more than hating them ever could. The most important thing about your job is you.

Have you ever noticed, the harder you work, the farther you get behind? It's true, think about it. Here you are just chugging along working hard and someone approaches you and asks for help, and before you know it, you end up doing the job for them. Sound familiar? That's how others take advantage of you. Then management sees how hard you work and they'll just pile more on top of you until eventually you end up doing most of the tasks, meanwhile they get away with doing less and less work. That's why you never show how much you really are capable of doing.

Don't forget to pretend to be working hard. Remember to work smarter, not harder. Instead of walking or moving really fast, just pretend or make it appear that you are. To do this, use the slacking technique called "Baby Stepping". These are shorter, smaller, and slower steps which will make it look like you are walking fast even if you're not. Remember, if you have to ask for help, then that means you are either working too hard or not hard enough.

Also if you are not in a union, watch out for the employer's firing trick. It's that little small print that says that you were "hired at will" and can be "fired at will". Use that to your advantage when you have to quit.

Another tip for those of you who have to pretend to do physical work. Don't be afraid to sweat a little. Just splash some water on your head and shirt and let it drip down and make it appear that you are really working hard and sweating your "_ss off". That always works really well. And don't forget to drip a little under your arms too. Then drip all over the paper work or near others. Better yet, drip some sweat on them and then they'll leave you alone for sure. Pretend that you are breathing hard from working and breath on them. People don't want other people's breath and sweat on them. They'll be running away from you before you know it.

Always have a designated hiding spot where no one can see you. In fact, have several and don't forget to rotate as often as needed. It's also a very good idea to have a couple of other places that you can retreat to in case you are discovered. But, be careful not to be found out that you are slacking. Have something nearby and ready to go at ALL TIMES, in case someone finds you. Be ready to make it look like you are doing something, such as looking at a part, shuffling papers, or doing something that's work related. If at all possible, find a spot where you can see everyone else and what's going on. Basically just sit and watch everyone else work without them seeing you.

Don't forget to watch out for those pesky video cameras. They're popping up all over now because they are so cheap. Just remember, some are so small and can be hidden just about anywhere. That's why you have to fight back and get yourself a bug detector.

Bug detectors are cheap and can help you locate hidden wireless cameras that give off a radio frequency (RF) signal.

You don't want anyone getting you on tape while you are slacking. Remember, some cameras are not out in the open and often, aren't even visible. They can be very small and hidden in places that you may not expect to find one. Cameras can be hidden in clocks, fire alarms, vents, small holes in the wall, pictures, small hole in ceiling, light switches, etcetera.

So, if you are new on the job, look around and keep your eyes peeled for cameras. Check in ceilings, etcetera. And after a short while you'll know where the safe spots are. Pay attention to others and their habits and gossip. But don't let that discourage you from slacking. Often times, the cameras are management's way of using scare tactics. Many times they only view the cameras if something happens. The company usually gets a discount on their liability insurance rates just by installing them. Keep your eyes and ears open to where the cameras are being taped or DVR'd.

If you find the source, look at the angle of the cameras on the screen so you know all the blind spots. It will take several attempts to study the cameras. But don't study too much at one time or someone will get suspicious. Just glance at the monitor once in a while until you have learned the viewing angles. Look for the areas that are and are not being recorded or monitored. That will give you an idea where you can and can't slack.

Also, you can use the cameras to your advantage by knowing where they are being used. Every time you are in the cameras zone you can pick up the pace and walk a little faster until you are out of range. Then slow back down to baby stepping. While you are in range, you can make it appear that you are working. In fact, you should only do work while in the cameras range, and then slack when you're not in range. That way, if the camera's recordings are viewed it'll always look like you are busy.

Another good hiding place is in bathrooms. They are a relatively safe spot to get away from the worries of work. Sneak a magazine or a newspaper in with you so it helps pass the time. If by some chance you get interrupted or don't have time to finish reading your paper, just hide it behind the toilet or behind the garbage can. That way you can finish reading it later on. Never go to the bathroom on your breaks and lunches. Always go on their time. Drink lots of coffee or water. That way you have to keep going to the bathroom all the time and it helps keep you away from working. If they have a water cooler, drink their water. That's part of those creating your own benefits you read about earlier.

Talking about your personal life MUST be kept at a minimum or better yet, not at all. If you want to really have fun when someone asks about your personal life, just "bull-_hit" them all the time. Make stuff up about yourself and say different things about the same question all the time.

It'll confuse the "_ell" out of everyone once they start talking about you among themselves.

They won't be able to figure you out. Remember, they are all "bull_hitters" too. Remember this when talking, "You can't bullshit a bullshitter unless you're a better bullshitter than the bullshitter you're trying to bullshit." Oops! Besides, people don't need to know your personal life. More times than not, they'll use that against you in a sarcastic sort of way. The least they know about you the better. If they persist, then just keep it yes or no answers when asked. Talking about your personal life will come back to haunt you someday. You might mention something to someone and before you know it, everyone in the whole company knows your personal life.

Better yet, when they ask you a personal question, just respond by saying "Why do you want to know?" Then let them fumble about and it will put them on the spot.

Whatever their response is, just tell them "ohh you'll have to do better than that." Then just walk away leaving them hanging and they'll look more stupid than ever.

Sometimes they'll even have a "smart-_ssed" or sarcastic comment of their own. Some co-workers are just plain nosy and are nothing but busybodies. They'll make a comment just to get anyone to talk to them so they can find out info. An example of a comment one might say to you is "So, what do you know?" Just respond by saying "Too much!" Then walk away and let them find another victim. You have to be on the ball with this one. It's a trick question to make you look bad or stupid. Don't say "nothing", which is the most common response. Then they will always come back with a smart comment. That's how they try to set you up and get the better of you. That's why you need a comeback such as, "Too much!". They will have a hard time coming back with a smart comment.

People are very repetitive about almost everything in life. That's why you need to listen in on other peoples conversations and you'll hear what they say which will usually always be the same thing day after day, such as a greeting. Then you will have time to prepare what you are going to say to them when they approach you.

It's very important to stay on top of this so you can end the conversation before it even gets started. The biggest conversation starters are when co-workers or others see you for the first time of the day. They'll say those annoying and monotonous things everyday like "Good morning" or "Good afternoon". That's when you need to come up with something creative or different than everyone else. Respond back by saying "Top of the morning to you", or "Bottom of the afternoon to you". They won't know how to respond. They may even ask you if you're Irish. Then just respond by saying "I'm not at liberty to say" or "I plead the fifth".

It's important to keep walking as you talk to them or they'll want to have a conversation. You can also say, "How are you doing, that's swell glad to hear it" all at the same time while not even giving them a chance to talk or answer you. Just keep walking by them all in one motion. It'll make you look like you're much too busy to talk.

A disgruntled employee may say "they are there to work, not to make friends; they do their job, then go home". This is true about slacking, but again, you don't want to walk around looking like you are mad at the world. Then you look like you're disgruntled and that refers to step 2 of the game rules. Don't get mad or make it appear that you are disgruntled. Just pretend to be happy. If you find yourself too overwhelmed with anger and know you're not going to be able to control it, just walk away with a smile on your face and take a few deep breaths and continue on your business. It'll probably be the hardest thing to do while on your way to becoming a Slackmaster but you must not give in.

No matter how much you want to push someone's face to the back of their skull with your fist. Remember, control and deep breaths. As always, keep grinning. It makes people wonder what you are up to. You'll soon be able to pick them apart by being happy all the time.

When talking, if you try to stay on work related topics, they'll think that you really care about your job. It's all about faking and false impressions. Another good excuse to use to avoid conversation is to just say in a quiet voice "I've got a sore throat and it hurts too much to talk". Avoidance is always the best way to go, but sometimes you just don't have a choice and get cornered. If that happens, it's important to remember to just make them feel uncomfortable to be around you.

Try eating lots of garlic the night before and also before work. Then just breath on people and they'll usually go running. If you have to "_art", just let it fly and then blame it on them.

Another thing to remember is always deny everything and make counter acquisitions. If someone comes to you saying "you were supposed to have this done by now" Just respond by saying "I didn't know I was supposed to do it, I heard that Jim said he was going to do it". That's how you deny first, then make counter acquisitions. Even if there is nobody by the name of Jim that works there, that's fine because it sets you up to use the next technique.

Switch to the confusion technique if they are still persistent. To do this, you need to really confuse the "_ell" out of them. You might want to say "who did he tell you that to". Say it kind of fast so their brain cannot process what you just said. Then repeat it again if necessary. They won't know how to respond. Then say "oh no, I think I just sharted, I'll have to worry about that later." Then walk swiftly to the nearest bathroom so you can plan your next attack with how you're going to get out of it. It gives you time to calm down and get back into the negotiating scheme of things.

That's what car salesmen do when you are negotiating. When things get heated and they feel the pressure, they say that they have to go talk to their manager.

CHAPTER 4:

Workplace Problems a Slackmaster Might Encounter

It's just always a given that no matter where you work, there is always at least one stinky person you will have to work with. You can respond by saying, "Did something die, oh it's just your breath". Another big problem you'll have to face in the workforce is pay. There always seems to be someone else who does less work then you but gets paid much more. It's one thing if that person has been working there for many years and has a lot of experience and actually works hard. But it's a whole different story when someone who has been there for many years and still doesn't know their "_ss" from a hole in the ground and has no clue on how to do their job. Also, another problem can be if a new employee is paid as much or more than you. It's wrong, but it happens just about everywhere.

Let's face it, if someone has been working at the same place and putting up with the same crap for many years, he or she deserves to be compensated for it. And if that person happens to be you then that's when you need to create your own benefits.

Even if someone is very knowledgeable about their job, and works diligently and should therefore be deserving of a raise, most times they just "get screwed". Eventually, a person says to themselves, "Why bother". That's right, "Why bother". So once they come to that conclusion, there's only one thing left to do; "**Slack**". There's little that can be done about their pay, except to create their own benefits, which we'll talk about in a later chapter.

Don't show off or talk about things that you own. Let others see that you don't make enough money. Don't eat lunch with your opponent(s), instead, bring your lunch to work and eat it while you work, on their time of course.

Don't eat in front of others and don't let anyone see you eating. Not only will you benefit from saving money by brown bagging it for lunch, it gives you a way to use up those leftovers too. That way when lunch comes around, just sit around or read an old newspaper.

Read old newspapers that have been lying around. That way when someone asks why you don't eat lunch, you can reply by saying, "I sure would like to eat lunch but I can't afford to, I can't even afford to buy a current newspaper, I have to read an old one that's lying around and that's old news. But old news is new news to me!".

Here are a few common conversations people try to start. "Did you see such and such on TV last night?" Respond by saying, "I can't afford cable, I have an old 13 inch black and white that only gets 3 channels." or "I wish I could afford cable."

Another conversation starter that people try to use is when they try to show you something on their phone. Just respond by saying "Wow, you have a portable phone, I don't have one of those, I wish I could afford one of those cellular type devices".

Often others will try to talk to you about what they did the night before or on the weekend, when they say "Did you see such and such movie, I went and saw it and it was good." You can respond by saying, "Movie, I haven't seen a movie in 20 years. I can't afford to go see a movie on my meager salary."

And of course there's always the "I ate this last night" or "I ate at that new restaurant". You can respond by saying, "I can't afford to eat every day" or "I can't afford to eat out" or "Last night I had to make a choice between putting gas in my car or food." After while they'll get the hint that you don't care to hear about their gloating.

CHAPTER 5:

Picking Your Opponent Apart

If they sit down by you to eat lunch just say, "It sure must be nice to afford the luxuries of life, like food". Or you can say, "I'd eat lunch too, but I had to put gas in my car so I can come to work." Or while in the parking lot when someone pulls in and others are around say, "Gee, it must be nice to be able to afford a newer car." You'll think of many others along the way, just be sarcastic about it, nicely, not with an attitude.

That's why you should always drive a beater car to work. And when it comes to work related projects or activities, never use your own vehicle. When you arrive at work and park, that's where your vehicle should stay until it's time to go home. Why put extra wear and tear on your own vehicle? Let the ones making the big bucks use theirs.

If anyone asks, "What are you doing for lunch?", or asks, "Where are you going for lunch?" you can reply, "I can't afford to go out to lunch, I have to brown bag it." or you can say, "I can't afford to put any extra wear and tear on my vehicle".

Another good one is, "I have some problems with my car and can't afford to fix them and don't want to chance using it anymore that I have to". Then if they ask, "What's wrong with it?". Make something up such as, "I have no washer fluid and can't afford to buy a gallon of it" or "I have a brake light out and can't afford a bulb." Even if it is more convenient to drive to another building or area on the other side of a campus or parking lot, don't! Don't put the stress and extra wear and tear on your own vehicle, use a company vehicle or better yet just walk. That way, it will take up more time, and you'll also keep in shape.

When people at work see you pull up in an old beat up hoopty, rust falling off, exhaust leak, etcetera; you'll be surprised how no one will ever bug you for a ride to lunch or anywhere for that matter. Be sure to park it next to the bosses car too, who knows maybe they'll realize they aren't paying you enough. Or probably not.

It can't be emphasized enough; if others know your personal life, they'll use that against you and stab you in the back. Therefore, now it's time for you to turn the tables on them and use their chat about their personal lives to your advantage. When they start talking about what they had for dinner, then you can say, "I wish I could afford a steak for dinner", "maybe someday in the next couple of decades I'll be able to afford to eat out." When they talk about their new car or even one that's 10 years old, you can say, "It must be nice to be able to drive a newer car".

If they start talking about a vacation or something they've got, then respond by saying, "I wish I could afford to get a new toy, like a boat", "It must be nice to afford to take a trip or a vacation.", "I can only afford a stay-cation". Just remember, that if you talk about your personal life, they might say things like that back at you.

CHAPTER 6:

Defensive Slacking

Now it's time to learn about Defensive Slacking. The smart defensive slacker learns through lots of practice, to spot trouble while it is still some distance away. He or She should always make a concerted effort to get away from the area and avoid the trouble entirely. Within no time, you'll learn to avoid situations where trouble is likely to occur. For example, trouble could be your boss and other co-workers and hiding from them is your goal. Out of sight and out of mind. If you are hiding in a closet for example and you hear one of those pesky coworkers walk by, sneak out and move to another location. Always be ready to relocate at anytime. If you are on one side of a room or hallway and you see trouble, like your boss coming in the door, quickly go out another doorway.

Act like you never saw him or her, and don't acknowledge them either. Don't make eye contact or that'll be a sure sign of them knowing you know that they are there.

It's best to use the "Duck and Cover" technique. In other words, go out the opposite way and duck into the bathroom. Don't forget, sometimes these annoying coworkers will try to follow you and try to talk to you. However when and if that annoyance/trouble finds you, make sure you go into a stall in the bathroom. You have now run out of all Defensive techniques at this time. So now it's time to switch to a quick "Offensive" slacking technique.

If they are persistent on bothering you, even when you are in the stall, then every time they talk to you flush the toilet. You may have to do that several times. Eventually they will get the hint and that will make them go away. In most cases, you'll hear them say, "Ohh, never mind, I'll catch up with you later." When you find yourself cornered, make them feel embarrassed and extremely uncomfortable around you.

That's called the Offensive Slacking Technique. Remember, always try to use Defensive first and if that doesn't work, quickly switch to Offensive.

Sometimes you'll have to confront trouble face to face and it's always a good idea to practice your offensive techniques. Try to make the situation embarrassing for them. People will go out of their way to try and not get embarrassed. Humans hate to be embarrassed, so try to make them embarrassed as "_ell". When a coworker starts talking to you about what a wonderful weekend they just had, or they come to you with a problem; Yawn, yawn loudly and proudly. If they are very persistent and can't take a hint, start picking your nose or ear, or both. Then pretend to become fascinated by what's on your finger more than what they are saying.

If they still don't get the hint, Show off your prize
that's on your finger, hold it in front of them and say to
yourself out loud, but in a quiet voice just loud enough for
them to hear, "Wow look at this one." That will make them go
away. Because there are always a few brain dead people you
might have to work with, you might have to use the last resort,
just interrupt them and say, "I'm sorry did you say something?
I got to go take a dump."

Make them feel uncomfortable around you not just
once but every time, and soon you'll see them going out of
their way to avoid you. Embarrass them when they are around
others. When Bob is talking with others, just interrupt them by
saying, "Hey Bob, I heard about your hemorrhoids, I hope you
get over that." If you are questioned about it, just say you
heard it from Jim. Put the blame on someone else. Sometimes
you need to turn defensive slacking into offensive slacking.

Here's the same example again. You are walking by Bob while he is talking to others and he or one of the others say something to you first, then you may feel the need to switch to offense by saying, "Hey Bob, I heard about your hemorrhoids, I hope you get over that." In time, slacking will be nothing more than routine, and by turning slacking into a routine, it will help make the day go by faster as well.

Always be aware of your surroundings and keep track of other people and their habits and what routines they are in. That way you'll be able to plan your slacking routine accordingly. Remember, just about everyone has some kind of routine. Some may go to the bathroom around the same time or take breaks or talk to someone around the same time. Just make a mental and physical note of that for future reference.

Don't leave any written notes about peoples routines lying around. Take it home with you each day. Someone may find your notes and learn your techniques and that will definitely come back to haunt you. If they would find your notes around the workplace about peoples comings and goings, and habits they might think that you are plotting a terrorist attack. You know how paranoid and scared everybody is now a days.

Soon you'll have many new techniques to try on people.

CHAPTER 7:

Create Your Own Benefits

After you are truly into a slacking routine, you will get

to know the sounds of certain peoples shoes, voices, which

door just shut, etcetera. It'll seem like you are living the same

day over and over. However, don't let that get you down.

Use the monotony to your advantage by bringing

magazines, newspapers, and books to read. Bring a cooler or

briefcase to work and keep little things to do in it. Also, make

sure you always bring all of your personal things home with

you EACH day. Do all the little things you just don't have

time to do at home, like cleaning your golf clubs, cutting and

filing your nails, or shaving your face and or legs. When you

are truly into a slacking routine, you will be able to do all those

little time consuming things at work that you just don't have

time to do at home.

By doing as many personal things at work as you can (while slacking), that will leave more time for you at home. In other words, why spend hours of reading at home when you can do it at work. That way you'll have more time to watch the TV program you always miss, do chores, or even get that full nights rest you so deserve.

Here are a few bonus tips to do while creating your own benefits while slacking:

If you have to ask for help that means you are working too hard.

Talk on your cell phone but while bending down to make it look like you are looking for something.

Clean your shoes at work. You must have stepped in something in the parking lot. That way it'll help make you look more presentable.

It's a good idea to have both of your hands full. That way if anybody says, "Can you give me a hand?", you can say, "Sorry my hands are full".

Hold doors open for people. Not only will people think you are being kind, but it also wastes time.

Here's one learned from a big administrative person making $120,000 a year. Walk around with a piece of paper in your hand to look important. And remember, if anyone asks it's a document, not a paper.

Cleaning Tips

When cleaning areas with moveable furniture, spill pop or something sticky or just don't clean the floor for a while. That way the furniture will stick to the floor and when people sit, they sometimes drop change from their pockets in between the furniture and they'll think the furniture doesn't move. Then all you have to do is move the furniture and collect the money. Now that's a benefit that only you can create.

When Vacuuming, you might accidently suck up things like change, jewelry or maybe that nice pen on a desk, accidently of course. Later, when you can change the bag and it accidently rips open, you can collect your rewards of labor.

Don't clean windows every day. Do them once a week. When you do clean them, it'll make a big difference and you'll get noticed for sure. If you are questioned on dirty areas, just say the cobwebs and dust is creating a SPF of 10 to help with the fading effects from the sun.

Other Tips

Don't forget, when you are given a task to do with a company vehicle, use it for your personal use too. Stop and get that lotto ticket instead of doing it after work on your time. Or perhaps even picking up the kids from school, or snow plowing your own driveway with a company vehicle, or going home for lunch with a company vehicle.

Why not take that vehicle to the store and do a little shopping while you're at it. If you are hungry, stop and get something to eat, all on their time.

Tips to keep you safe and healthy

When lifting heavy objects that requires 2 or more people, let the others do all the lifting. Just lift a little to make it look like you are doing you share. To make it really look authentic, make faces and grunting sounds. That way, others will really think you are doing most of the lifting. But, don't be over dramatic about it. Don't forget, work smarter, not harder. The key to successful slacking is good acting. So not only are others thinking that you are working, but you'll get to polish up on those acting skills of yours as well.

Remember that acting is not acting when you are by yourself, so always make guest appearances every once in a while and let people see you working. In other words, don't hide all day. Make a guest appearance once in a while. That way people will see that you are there and "working", but just for a couple of minutes at a time; otherwise, they might want you to do something for them.

When someone starts to ask you something, immediately interrupt them. Distract the supervisor or any coworker for that matter by talking about something not work related, such as the weather, some ball game, etcetera. Many people only have the ability to keep one topic in their thoughts, and once you interrupt them they'll forget what they were going to ask you. However don't forget, when something is on their mind, they won't listen to you because they know they'll end up losing their thought.

They'll try to say it right when you stop talking. So go on to another subject two or three times, and finally follow it up with a question. And by that time, they would have forgotten their thought. But beware, they might come back as soon as they remember their thought, so use the "Duck and Cover" technique.

CHAPTER 8:

Fifty Excuses For Calling In Sick

One of the most popular ways of slacking at work is not to go to work... However, don't waste a sick day when you are sick, save them for nice days or use them on a Monday or Friday or both. That way you have a longer weekend. If you really are feeling under the weather, don't be miserable at home when you can be miserable at work. Always try to go to work when you are sick; that way it gives you an excuse to slow down at work. If you do end up needing an excuse, then a cold is always a good one to use while slacking. If you happen to get others sick at work because of your cold, that is a big plus because that gives them more incentive to take a sick day. Then it doesn't look like you are the only one using sick days. When others are sick, that gives you an opportunity to call in sick too. Not only will less actual work get done, it helps to create job security.

After all, where do you think you got the cold from to begin with? You probably got it from the work place anyway; now it's time to return the favor.

Often times, people lose much of their sick time when they retire, quit, or get fired. So you might as well use it up. Some employers offer to buy back your accumulated sick time when you retire at a much reduced rate and often times have a cap on that. If you work at a place for 20 or more years and save most of your sick time, it's not uncommon to have two or three hundred or more sick days saved up. If you retire and they only give you $20 for each unused sick day, you are getting ripped off. Those sick days are worth a lot more than $20 if you were to call in sick and get paid for the day.

If you make $80 a day and get paid $10 an hour and they are only offering you $20 for each sick day, it's like getting paid $2.50 an hour. That's not only an insult, it's also stupid. Your time is worth a lot more than $2.50 an hour.

Here's an example: Jim earns $15 an hour and has worked for a place for 30 years and has 315 accumulated sick days when he retires. His employer encourages their employees not to use their sick time because they will pay you for your unused sick days when you retire.

Sounds great until Jim retires and finds out that over his 30 years of employment at his job, his company has changed the polices many times about sick time and retirement. His, like most employers will only pay $20 per day and up to a $5000 cap. That means that Jim will only be paid for 250 of his sick days, thus losing 65 of them. That's $2.50 an hour for 2000 hours.

Jim thinks that's ok; he's still getting $5000. What Jim didn't realize is that he has been screwed over by his employer. Jim could have gotten $15 an hour for 2,520 hours. Which would translate to a loss of $37,800 for his sick time if he had used up his time and called in sick. This is one of many ways that employers are screwing their workers.

If they were paying you time for time it would be a different story, however you know very few employers do that. Here's a parting thought on sick days in rough economic times like these. If you quit or get fired, you will lose them all. Use them before you lose them. So get on the phone and call in sick.

50 Excuses for calling in sick.

1. **My hair hurts** (after getting a haircut, I should stay home and count my hair)

2. **I got crabs and diarrhea** (we won't go there)

3. **I got cramps and gas** (let it rip, in the background)

4. **I got a bad case of Jock itch today** (nothing better than scratching yourself all day)

5. **I got toe fungus** (kick back and scratch your feet)

6. **I got athletes foot** (it may hurt to walk around)

7. **I got an upset stomach** (vomiting always works)

8. **I got a stomach ache** (must have been something I ate)

9. **I got a headache** (must be from that beer last night)

10. **I got a migraine** (must be from that 12 pack last night)

11. **I got pink Eye** (must have scratched my eye with dirty hands)

12. **My grandmother died** (make sure she doesn't die 3 or 4 times, otherwise they might become suspicious)

13. **I have a sore throat** (make sure you cough a few times while calling in sick)

14. **I lost my voice** (make sure you whisper when calling in)

15. **My car won't start** (must be that damn battery again)

16. **My tire fell off while driving to work** (oops)

17. **My kid/s sick** (even if you don't have any)

18. **My dog is sick** (have to take my fish to the vet)

19. **My grandfather died** (make sure you don't use this one more that 3 or 4 times)

20. **My Parent is sick and in the hospital** (come up with a new disease)

21. **I got a killer hang nail** (them things are a "_itch")

22. **I got an ingrown toe nail** (hurts doesn't it?)

23. **I have a huge zit on my forehead** (it'll be too embarrassing to come in)

24. **My hemorrhoids are flaring up** (I bet they are, have a seat)

25. **I got a case of insomnia** (I couldn't sleep a wink last night)

26. **I got the flu** (this works great after a few cases at work are reported)

27. **I got the flu again** (good for 48 hrs)

28. **Someone stole my car** (oh wait I found it)

29. **I lost my car keys** (good thing you found them in time to go to work the next day)

30. **My car won't make it thru the snow** (it's stuck)

31. **My water pipe bust last night** (it'll take all day to clean up)

32. **My herpes outbreak is acting up again** (they might tell you to take a few days off)

33. **I got the sniffles** (try to hold back a sneeze while calling in)

34. **My washer broke and I don't have any clean clothes** (I hate that, Mr. Stinky)

35. **My dryer broke and I don't have any dry clothes** (you're all wet)

36. **The laundry mat was closed/robbed last night** (I can't afford to buy my own washer and dryer)

37. **My skins itching all over** (try using soap next time you bathe)

38. **I got a rash** (let them guess where)

39. **If you are a female say "I got female problems"** (they won't even ask)

40. **I woke up feeling real achy** (you'll need to stay in and rest)

41. **I spilled scolding coffee on myself and got a 2nd degree burn** (If they ask, it was in your lap)

42. **I got a nasty paper cut** (and it hurts like "_ell")

43. **I accidentally sprayed deodorant in my eyes** (I can't see good enough to drive to work)

44. **I cut myself shaving** (where were you shaving)

45. **I ate a garlic meal last night and I stink because it's coming out of my pours** (stinky "_astard")

46. **I ate something that didn't agree with me last night** (you could have the "_hits" or sharts)

47. **I think I got food poising** (must have been that raw meat)

48. **I dropped a can of creamed corn on my toe** (toe's work great because there's nothing that can heal them, just time)

49. **I cut my finger with a knife while making my lunch** (make sure you put a band aid on the next day)

50. **I feel light headed and dizzy** (what were you smoking)

Bonus 51.   **I closed my finger in my car door this**

morning (before or after you locked it)

These are just a few of the top reasons to call in sick to

work and I'm sure you can think of many more.

CHAPTER 9:

Revenge, A Dish Which Is Best Served Cold

You also want to try to avoid arguments with the boss because when you complain about something the boss will see you as a bad influence with a bad attitude, and will usually try to get you to change your attitude by rewarding you with, yep you guessed it, with more work. Sometimes being a slacker means swallowing your pride. It's ok to put your 2¢ in once in a while, but don't appear to be mad or disgruntled. There are other things you can do by creating your own benefits.

Some examples of creating your own benefits might be, taking extended lunches or breaks, doing stupid things that might cost the company money, like breaking something or dumping a three hundred dollar gallon of chemical down the drain, accidentally of course. "Oops it slipped out of my hand, just call me mister butterfingers." Act your wage.

Flicking a light switch on and off or putting the switch half way up is another good way because some of the older switches will sometimes spark and short out sometimes causing a fire. Now I'm not suggesting you go burn your place of employment down, just do things that will cost them in the long run. Flush that toilet three, six, or maybe twelve times instead of once. Take several minutes to wash your hands, using Hot water of course. Someone has to pay that water bill.

Use paper towels and the electric hand dryer. Screw up multiple copies at the copy machine; it wastes toner, electricity, and paper. When cleaning, be sure to use extra chemicals and take extra care not to spill most of it down the drain (hint). Double or triple the amount of plastic bags you use and change the trash often, even when it has just one thing in it.

Leave lights on where ever possible. And if you are lucky enough to get to use a company car, the possibilities are endless. Ever wonder what would happen if you put a car in park while driving down the road? Ever wonder how fast a car will stop when put into reverse while driving down the road? Management does these things all the time such as using a company vehicle to run errands and to do some personal things too, like stopping at a store on the way or as mentioned before, picking up the kids from school, or using a company snow plow to remove the snow from your own driveway.

Also, driving a company vehicle home for lunch so that they don't waste their own gas. Buy things on the companies' expense account for themselves. If management can do these things, so can you. It would have been much cheaper for them to have given you that raise you deserved. And remember to **slack, slack, slack.**

Slacking is creating your own benefits. Even fringe benefits are hard to come by. So if your employer offers a free meal at a meeting, take advantage of it. Go up for seconds and thirds. Especially at Christmas parties, if it's on their tab, order the most expensive thing on the menu. And when free drinks are offered, drink up. If you don't drink alcohol, then drink as much pop as you can and if you don't feel like drinking too much, just keep getting as many drinks as possible and feed it to the plants or down the drain in the bathroom. Might as well, it's free and when an employer gives anything free take as much as you can as fast as you can. Order a drink (the expensive ones) take one sip, set it down somewhere and then go order another one. Do that as much as you can. Most of the time people are walking around talking anyway, so just leave your drinks at other people's tables.

If asked, always say that it takes longer to do something than it really does. Therefore, this can justify and accounts for the time spent slacking. Of course, this is harder to do when you have a strict quota to meet. That's why factory work is by far the hardest job to slack at. Especially when working on an assembly line. Try to avoid these types of jobs at all cost since most of these jobs are going overseas anyway and are paying minimum wage. Just remember, you get what you pay for and that goes for employers too.

Let's put it into another perspective. Procrastination Slacking. When slacking, procrastination is the king of all that you see. Here is how procrastination can pay off in the slacking world. If you are asked to do a project, especially a difficult one that you don't want to do, and you can't get motivated to get it started, then immediately start doing something else, taking your mind completely off the project at hand.

To be successful at procrastination slacking, you need to take your mind off the main project and do whatever it is that you would normally be doing. Even though you subconsciously know you should be working on the main task. Instead of dwelling on the first project, just go on to something else and keep doing that over and over moving on to other things. Then when asked if you finished that project you can say, "I have been so busy doing all these other things." After a while you might get lucky and they will stop giving you the big projects and move on to someone else.

CHAPTER 10:

Team Slack

This chapter goes against the Slackmaster's code of ethic and most Slackmaster's will never use the techniques in chapter 10, so therefore, it must be used with extreme caution. It's hard to trust others, in fact you never should, but once in an extremely great while you'll find someone in the same situation as you and become a team. Team Slack. Team slack will only be someone you truly trust such as a spouse or family member or close friend outside of work. You have been warned to take caution and it is not advisable to form a team, but sometimes on rare occasions it can work out. When talking among other co slack partners, be ready to change the subject immediately in case another coworker stumbles upon you and make sure your slack partner knows this so when you change the subject they take that as a cue. Always change to a work related project or topic.

77

Talk in odd areas like a restroom, but not stalls because someone could walk in and you'll never know it, and be careful in hallways, someone could be around a corner when sharing slacking ideas.

Always be prepared for someone to walk in on you and have a backup plan ready for when they do. You might have to even start walking and talking, depending on the situation. It might make it look better to even appear to be working. Talking can always eat up a lot of time; but remember to use this technique wisely because talking can make or break you when it comes to slacking. This can't be stressed enough, Don't talk out in the open where others can see you.

One of the best ways to slack, but not widely used is to slack with the boss. Yes, that's right, the enemy! It's a gutsy but bold move that has to be very well scouted before undertaking a task as such.

As the old rule of thumb goes, sometimes it's best to have an enemy you know rather than one you don't. Talking with the boss is also another great way to kill time.

However, caution should be used and should only be done by a true Slackmaster, and watch what you say because they might be setting you up. Ask him or her questions about a work related project or anything work related. You will be able to slack right under your bosses' nose without them even knowing what you are really up to.

Then talk about the weather or something not work related just to kill more time. That way if asked where you were you can say you were talking to the boss about a particular project. Of course, this depends on the particular boss; not all are the same or easy to talk to. Let's face it, most are just plain "_ssholes" on an ego trip just because they have power. After all, putting in your time is all you have to do, and by slacking it creates job security because there will always be something to do.

If you bust your "_ss" and finish a task, too early and are standing around, management will be wondering if they should cut another job and/or give you more work to do.

This is especially true with state and government jobs because they are always looking for ways to cut jobs, and by cutting jobs, management gets a bigger bonus.

CHAPTER 11:

Stupidity Should Hurt, Bad!

Let's face it, most of the people we work with are nothing more than a bunch of brain dead, "kiss _ss", morons. Some are so stupid, you wonder how they even remember to breath. They are constantly sticking their foot in their mouth and are constantly hurting themselves physically. Well, you know what? Stupidity should hurt! Now, it's time to have fun and take advantage of the stupidity at the work place. Always tell everyone something completely different about something. It confuses them.

When asked about a certain job, task, or anything at all, **Always** and this cannot be stressed any more, always say, "I don't remember" or "I can't recall." It will usually get you off the hook. After all, it worked for a former President of the United States.

It works for all those crooked politicians when they are in trouble or on trial. Another thing to Remember to say is. "I honestly can't remember." or "Not that I can recall".

When some moron is down, kick them again, it's fun and makes the day go by faster. You may not mean to laugh at the misfortune of others, but it's so easy. They're so stupid. After all, they would do the same to you, especially the ones who get special treatment and more pay then you do and are only expected to do the very least.

Just remember, stupidity is rarely disciplined by the employer!

Here are a few examples of stupidity in which all of these examples are true and really occurred at various work places:

A Public works supervisor worker: Instead of using wire or zip ties to hang a banner from a street light, the supervisor wanted his workers to use baggie ties.

Same public worker: When hanging a banner and sign for an important event be sure to tie it to something classy, like a trash can. Done also by the supervisor.

A comment said to a maintenance worker by his boss in a building: "There are bugs in that light fixture, people might see that and get sick."

A painter: To save money, the painter used non-washable paint to paint the walls of a public school building. That way the scuff and dirt marks can be easily removed when wiped off; along with the paint too. Now that's job security.

At a local gym: A person working out decided to charge their cell phone with a wall outlet located in the main hallway. When they walked away they were asked if they were worried about it getting stolen.

Same gym five minutes later: Person puts a cardboard box over the phone while it's charging that way it won't stand out. Then walks away.

A janitor: was asked to put out a smoldering ash tray container outside an entryway. In order to put out the smoldering ash tray, the janitor brings the smoldering bucket of ash into the building and walks down the hall with it into the janitors' closet to put it out in the sink. There was so much smoke that it set off the fire alarms.

Same janitor: Tried to change the toilet paper in the bathroom and called his boss for help because he couldn't find the beginning of the roll.

And they keep 'em on the payroll. This just goes to show how stupidity rarely gets disciplined. Some of these persons continue to go on day after day doing the "unthinkably stupid" and go on to work many years and retire from places of employment. Stupid works for some people. Only some people don't have to fake it, they just are.

CHAPTER 12:

Victim Of Your Own Success

Don't be a victim of your own success. Fact: In prison you get time off for good behavior. At work you get rewarded for good behavior with more work. Think about it for a second. In other words, if you work too hard you'll end up having to work harder. Don't let them or anyone take advantage of you. Slacking is all about cutting corners where ever possible. You'll also be amazed and even shocked at how many corners you can get away with cutting. In no time you'll be saying to yourself, "I can't believe I used to do it that way before; it took me all day to do that. Now I can get it done in an hour." But don't let them see how fast it can get done by cutting corners. Otherwise, they'll pile more work on top of you. Never reveal your secrets to corner cutting to any of your coworkers, ever. Because in a second, they'll stab you in the back, no matter how much you think they are your friend.

They'll take your corner cutting idea straight to the boss in hopes of being rewarded for an idea that wasn't even theirs to begin with. They'll even kiss the bosses "_ss" and brown nose so much; they'll be able to see out the boss's mouth.

By no means are you to bring any cost cutting or time saving techniques to the boss either. It may just back fire and they'll dump a bigger work load on your lap, since you have extra time now. You might just cost cut you own job right out the door. Keep all your ideas to yourself. After all, who's going to benefit from the savings? It sure won't be you!!! You won't see any extra money in your check, that's for sure. Now turn the tables and use that extra time for yourself not them.

CHAPTER 13:

Typical Days Of Slacking

Slacking can be applied to just about any job out there. Sometimes you can start slacking right away at a new job. Other times it may take as long as a year before you get to learn the ins and outs and when to use the correct slacking techniques.

Slacking, after time, should become routine. You should not feel guilty at anytime for what you are, or aren't doing. If at any time you find yourself feeling bad about slacking or your actions, you need to remember that most employers can care less about you. All they care about is lining their own pockets. If you still fell guilty then it might be time to think about whether or not you are cut out to be a Slackmaster. A Slackmaster should never feel guilt or remorse about slacking. Just keep remembering that it's all a game.

89

Management doesn't feel any guilt or remorse when they lay people off. Management can care less about paying you a crappy wage and how you have to struggle paycheck to paycheck to get by. Just remember that ALWAYS, while slacking. There's no guilt in slacking.

Here are a few examples of a typical day of slacking for various slack jobs. These may give you some ideas and maybe you're already doing some of these. You'll read about Jane the secretary, Harry the janitor, and Josie the head of HR management.

Here's a typical work day for slacker Jane, an administrator assistant (secretary).

6:30 AM   Jane wakes up and gets ready to go to work.

She takes her time and then walks into her

office everyday at around 7:55, which is

planned that way. Her normal time to start is 8

AM. She takes special care to make sure she

never arrives late. If she arrives too early they

might expect her to start working right away. If

she does happen to arrive at work a little early,

she would just wait in her car and read a paper

or listen to the radio until it was time to start

work. Also it's very important that she takes

extra care not to arrive late either. Otherwise

that gives them something they can use against

her at a later date.

8:00 AM   When Jane gets to her desk or cubical she makes herself comfortable by going and getting a cup of coffee. Jane usually tries to make the coffee in the morning right away because she can kill about 10 minutes of time right off the bat. Plus, she can make it to her own liking. May times she receives complements such as, "Oh thanks for making the coffee Jane". When it comes to the morning coffee in an office environment, she will look like a hero. While she's waiting for the coffee to finish brewing, she goes and retrieves her favorite coffee cup and rinses it out. She gets all her office papers settled in and makes it look like she's already been working.

8:20 AM   By 8:20 she finally has her first of many cups of

coffee and is ready to start her day. She starts

off by checking her messages and takes any

notes if needed. Even if she doesn't have any,

she makes it look like she does and holds the

phone like she's checking messages while

writing her grocery list down to make it appear

like she's taking notes.

8:30 AM   By 8:30 she is ready to return any of her phone

calls. Oh no, she's out of coffee, she needs to

go get herself another cup. Oh not again, she

takes the last cup and now she needs to make

more coffee.

8:45 AM	By 8:45 she's finally back at her desk. As the boss is walking by, she picks up the phone and shuffles some papers and finishes writing her grocery list that she started earlier. Now, after drinking her two cups of coffee, she has to go to the restroom. She takes her time and makes sure she uses plenty of hot water to wash her hands. It is imperative that she thoroughly and frequently washes her hands throughout the work day.
9:05 AM	When she returns to her desk at 9:05, she realizes that she's out of coffee again so she goes and gets another cup before returning those calls.

9:10 AM   At 9:10 she finally returns her first call and

checks her emails. She always talks nice to the

customers and chit chats a while with each of

them. If one has a question she says to them,

"Hold on a minute while I check the computer."

By the time she gets her first call done it's

already 9:30.

9:30 AM   That coffee is really going thru her and she goes

to the restroom again. When she gets back, she

checks her phone messages and emails again.

She returns a few quick calls and emails. She

organizes her desk and ohh jesh, it's 10:00

already. It's time for break.

10:15 AM	When she gets back from break at 10:15 she sees her boss left her a lot of paper work to do and file. She's getting kind of hungry, so she finishes any calls and emails as she snacks on some food. By ll:30 she has made all her calls and answered all her emails.
11:30 AM	Her boss asks if she had finished all that paper work yet. She replies by saying, "I've had so many calls and emails to return, I'll finish it first thing right after lunch." Meanwhile, she enters some of the paper work into the computer and discreetly eats her lunch. That way she doesn't have to waste her lunch time actually eating her lunch. She looks at the time and goes to the restroom again and before she knows it, it's lunch time already.
12:00 PM	She goes and takes her lunch and returns at 1:00.

1:00 PM	She returns at 1:00 only to find more paperwork, phone messages, and emails to take care of. She finishes the first batch of paper and then takes a restroom break.
2:00 PM	Now at 2:00 she realizes it's crunch time and finishes making all her calls and emails quickly. After another restroom break (pre break) she takes her break at 3:00.
3:15 PM	She hands the finished paper work back to her boss and tells the boss that she'll try to finish the rest of it today or first thing tomorrow. The boss wanted it all done today so the boss takes some of the workload off of Jane and delegates it to others.

3:20 PM   Now that some of her workload has been

            reduced she can take her time finishing what

            she has left and even manages to find time to fit

            another restroom break in to go trim and file her

            nails and finishes her work around 4:40.

4:40 PM   She gathers her things together, cleans and

            organizes her desk and takes one last restroom

            break before that long ride home. You guessed

            it, it's 5:00 and time to leave for the day.

Important tips for office work

Waste time by making coffee, frequent trips to the restroom, etcetera... Be creative.

Keep your desk area cluttered throughout the workday; that way it will look like you are swamped with work all day.

Never answer the phone right on the first ring. That tells whoever is on the other line that you aren't very busy. The longer you let it ring before answering it, the better. Maybe someone else might answer it.

Try to do most of your work right away. Just leave a little of each project unfinished, that way when someone asks you for help, you can say, "Ohh, I'd like to, but I have a lot of projects that I'm working on that need finishing."

Finish your work at the end of the day. It shouldn't take too long since you already did most of it earlier and only have a little left to do. That way the boss will see you struggling to finish up at the end and maybe the boss won't give you so much work to do.

When you aren't busy, it's very important to look busy. Pick up the phone and dial the weather station. That way the boss will see the line is in use and will think that you are busy. You'll be able to hang up at anytime if someone should become suspicious. Talk once in a while to at least make it look like you are working. Shuffle paperwork or anything to make it appear that you are busy.

Again, be creative and you'll be able to come up with all kinds of ways to waste time, other than doing actual work.

Here's a typical work day for slacker Harry, who is a janitor.

A typical day for Harry consists of doing as little as possible. Harry knows that a janitor is a very low paying job and any hard work is never rewarded with any monetary value at all. There is no bonus or raise given to hard workers. The most he'll receive once in a while is a complement. Big deal, talk is cheap and worthless. If hard work was really appreciated, then it would be rewarded monetarily. So because of that, Harry does just what he has to in order to get buy.

10:50 PM   Harry's shift starts at 11:00, however, he always

arrives five minutes early so that no one could

ever say he's late. When he arrives, he

immediately goes into slack mode and starts his

routine. Harry always remembers the three

main things to always do and that's trash,

restrooms, and floors. Those are what most

people look for and would complain about. He

then gets his cart ready full of supplies and

heads out on his 8 hour slack journey. He

dumps all the trash first; that way if he finds

anything that he likes or can sell for money, he

takes it out to his vehicle right away. As he's

going through collecting the trash, he can get a

good idea of what he is in for that night.

11:45 PM   Harry is done with the trash and then takes a

half hour restroom break. He's always clever to

be seen as little as possible by other co-workers.

12:15 AM   Harry heads to the restrooms and remembers

that, if it looks good to him it'll look good to

others. In other words, he'll clean just enough

to make it appear to be clean, even thou the

littlest effort went into cleaning it. He starts by

cleaning the mirrors because that's the first sign

of a dirty restroom. After that, he uses the same

rag to clean the whole room. He starts with the

sinks by just doing a quick wipe down, then

moves on to the tops of the urinals and any

noticeable marks on the walls or partitions.

Next, he dumps or sprays some cleaning

chemicals in the toilets and urinals and leaves it

in to make it appear they were cleaned and

scrubbed. He notices that one toilet is dirty in

the bowl that wasn't able to come clean by 1 or 2 dozen flushes. So he only scrubs that one and wipes all the tops of the seats and toilets all with the same towel that he has been using since he started his shift.

He then moves onto the urinals for a quick wipe and he's all done. Next, he changes any paper towels and toilet paper, followed by picking up any noticeable garbage on the floor. Since he only sweeps and mops the floor about once every week or two instead of wasting time doing it every day like they think he's doing. That way it saves him a lot of time for his own personal time and breaks. He does a final walk through and realizes he wasted 20 minutes cleaning the restrooms.

The restrooms look good, the germs might still be there, but at least they look clean and that's all that matters.

12:35 AM   Harry then grabs a coffee from his lunch box and reads a magazine for about an hour.

1:35 AM   Harry takes another restroom break and then gets right back to work

2:00 AM   He quickly sweeps up the floors and dust mops the larger areas. Harry notices some spills on the floor, so he grabs a wet mop and just spot mops the spills, spots, and high traffic areas only. Since he only mops the hard floors once every week or two instead of every day, it saves him a lot of time. On the days he does his bi-weekly mopping, he'll just let something else go; that way it won't cut into his own time or his pre-breaks, breaks, pre-lunches, lunches, post lunches, or post breaks.

3:00 AM	By 3:00 Harry is starting to feel a little tired, so he goes and takes a nap for a while using the hide and go sleep technique. (Which you'll read about in the next chapter)
4:00 AM	When Harry wakes up, he sees he slept through his pre-lunch so he decides it's time to take lunch.
4:45 AM	Harry grabs his vacuum and cleans the carpet. He takes special care only to vacuum the big stuff that he sees; there's no need to vacuum the entire carpet. Each time he vacuums he picks a different wall and vacuums along the edges. He thanks the ants by the kitchen/break room because the ants pick up all the food debris and carry it into the edge of the wall for him where he can just vacuum it right up.

5:45 AM	Harry now takes his break and catches up on some much needed reading.
6:15 AM	Harry does some miscellaneous dusting and gets all the noticeable cob webs and dusty areas.
6:30 AM	Some of the early workers are starting to arrive to work, so Harry does the last thing before he winds down for the day. He cleans the windows and glass all over. He sprays very little and wiping quickly. He knows if he sprays too much it'll take him a lot longer to clean the windows and it'll streak and cut into his wind down time. Now that the others are arriving, they see him scrambling to finish up and they say to themselves, "Wow, look at Harry go, he's such a good worker."

6:45 AM   Now that Harry has made his guest appearance, he retreats to his closet and winds down for the day.

7:00 AM   Harry leaves and goes home after another rough day on the job.

Important tips for Cleaning

When carrying a bag of trash, don't squish the air out, instead fill it with air, it will look like it's fuller that it really is and heavier too.

And if you have to clean something, remember if it looks good to you, it'll look good to everyone else. It's all about looks. You can't see germs.

If you see something on the floor, just ignore it and pretend you never saw it. If you look at it as you walk by and don't pick it up, someone might see you and think that you are too lazy to pick it up.

If a floor is wet or there is a puddle on the floor, why waste time working by mopping it up, just put a wet floor sign on it. It will dry up eventually.

When cleaning, let some things go for a while. For example, don't wash windows every day, and then when you do decide to do them, you can do a real "half-_ssed" job because anything that you do will look better than what they were before.

The same goes for Vacuuming, let it go. Then, once in a while just vacuum the big things that are noticeable. Anything that you happen to vacuum would be an improvement from what it was. When someone walks by, they will see that you vacuumed and wouldn't even notice all the little debris left behind.

Cleaning is nothing more than an Illusion. If they think it's clean, then it's clean. What they don't know won't hurt them. Sometimes you have to let them sweat it out, they'll see the floors getting dirty and windows getting hand prints all over them. Then when it really gets bad, just do a quick and fast cleaning and they'll never know or notice all the things that you missed. In fact, you might even get complements.

Here's a typical work day for slacker Josie, who is head of HR management.

6:30 AM   Josie wakes up and gets ready to go to work. She takes her time and arrives at work a little late everyday at around 8:05, which she doesn't care since she is a boss and can get away with it.

8:05 AM   Josie tries to make sure she gets her coffee first before anyone else since it is already made. She forwards all her calls to her secretary and rushes to her first meeting of the day.

8:10 AM   Josie arrives late to her meeting which isn't a

big deal since all the other members of

management are arriving to the meeting at the

same time as she is. She and the rest of the

management team sit around and talk about

what they did over the weekend and then about

the weather. They need to kill some time since

they all have their schedules blocked off for 2

hours for this meeting.

8:35 AM   The members of management finally get the

meeting underway about some of the poor

morale in the other departments. They all agree

that since all their employees are getting a

dollar more an hour than minimum wage,

money can't be the issue for the poor morale

and it must be the workers themselves.

They decide that they can't decide what to do and will have to schedule another meeting to discuss it further. Then Josie talks about how she bought a new SUV and that it's the same model as what Phil the vice president just bought, only a darker color. They then take a break and get more coffee and go to the restroom. Soon they return and try to agree on a day to set the next meeting. Josie and the other managers pull out their so called smart phones and compare the phones and talk about some of the features. After that, they all look at their schedules and decide on the next meeting date, then depart.

10:15 AM   Josie finishes the meeting a little late, but that's ok, there's only 20 people waiting outside to use the room for their 10:00 meeting.

10:20 AM   Josie arrives back to her office after a much needed restroom break. She checks her phone messages and emails and forwards all of them to her secretary and tells her to call and email all of them back since she doesn't have time to do it.

10:30 AM   Josie calls her boy friend at home and discuses when he is going to marry her since they have been going and living together for 15 years.

10:40 AM   Josie forwards her calls to her secretary again and gets more coffee and is off to her other meeting that she wanted to have.

10:45 AM   Josie is waiting for the people to finish leaving

the room who had a meeting scheduled from 10

AM to 10:45 but had to finish their meeting

early since they couldn't get into the meeting

room on time at 10AM because of Josie's

meeting running 15 minutes over.

10:46 AM   Josie is furious because she had to start her

meeting 1 min late and wants to set up a future

meeting to discuss the proper use of time for the

meeting room. She pulls out her phone and sets

a date for that meeting. Josie and the others in

the meeting decide that would be a good idea

for a future meeting and should also have a

meeting about people taking long lunches too.

Now, they discuss what the afternoon meeting

is going to be about.

11:45 AM   The meeting ends and Josie goes to lunch

1:25 PM	Josie returns from lunch and checks her phone messages and emails and forwards them all to her secretary to handle since she's got a big meeting at 2:00. She asks her secretary to get all the details together for the meeting.
1:45 PM	Josie goes to the restroom, gets more coffee, and tells her secretary to hurry up with the reports. Josie gives her secretary more reports to enter into the computer for tomorrow's meeting.
2:00 PM	Josie and her management team arrive at the meeting to discuss how to deal with the back log of work that needs to be done. Josie says there is too much work that needs to be done and wants her managers to find out why it isn't getting done. Josie and her management team decide on when to have a follow up meeting on that matter. Then take a break.

2:50 PM   Josie and her team get back from a well

               deserved break after all of the tough decisions

               they just had to think about. Next they move on

               to a way for cost cutting and decide that the best

               way would be to freeze upcoming raises and cut

               a few jobs. Josie says that no one should be

               getting a raise in these tough economic times.

               Her team agrees. They take another break.

3:30 PM   Josie and her team are back to discuss how

               much of a raise to give Josie and her

               management team. They all agree that if they

               cut some wages, freeze raises and cut a few

               jobs, then the board of directors will agree to

               the raises for Josie and her management team.

3:55 PM	The meeting ends and Josie quickly goes back to her office and has her secretary type up a report to give to the board of directors on how she and her management team came up with ideas to save the company money and propose a raise for her and her management team.
4:30 PM	Josie goes to the meeting with the board of directors and discusses her proposals that her management team came up with to save money and give raises to her and her management team. The board agreed that the proposal for cost saving would be a good idea but want to change Josie's job title so that they could still justify giving her a 7% raise and freeze the wages of everyone else. She agrees and they vote on it unanimously.
4:50 PM	The meeting ends and Josie is happy about her big raise and goes home for the day.

Important tips for managers

Not all, but most managers are some of the biggest slackers in the world. That's how they got to where they are.

Set up as many meetings as you can; that way you don't have to do any work. All you have to do is just sit and discuss your personal lives and the newest thing you bought.

Delegate all you work to your secretary; that way you won't have to do any work whatsoever.

Forward all your calls and emails to your secretary and make him or her do all your dirty work by calling people back and sending emails.

Take long lunches and arrive late and leave early. No one will say anything, you're the boss.

Be as arrogant as you can and look down upon people as peasants. After all, mommy and daddy paid for you to go to college so you are better than everyone else.

As you can tell, the story about a typical work day for slacker Josie, who is head of HR management, is just a truthful example of how many, but not all members of management, get away with so much. The important tips are also an example how managers think of themselves and act.

CHAPTER 14:

Hide And Go Sleep

Another great way to pass the time at work is by sleeping. Let's face it; most people just don't get enough sleep, especially today with everyone's busy schedules. Working really cuts into a person's day, leaving very little time to get a full nights rest. Sleeping or taking naps during the day is not only healthy for you, but can leave you feeling more rejuvenated for your own personal time. Work is what's causing you to be tired, so why not sleep at work on their time and their dime. You must be warned, sleeping or napping during the work day can be habit forming on your body and you might find yourself needing to take a nap even on your days off.

Now, let's play hide and go sleep shall we? You'll
have to be very creative in the places where you rest, nap, or
sleep. Try to find a quiet place like in the restroom, a janitor's
closet, in the rafters or ceiling, in a car, under a desk. The
possibilities are endless. There is just one more important
thing and perhaps the most important thing, and that's not to
get caught. However, there are a few slacking techniques and
ways around getting caught and what to say if you do, which
you'll read about in a moment.

If you are the type that tends to fall into a deep sleep
easily, then you might want to only do so, on your actual
breaks and lunches; that way you can't get into trouble if
caught. Always have a pen and paper handy nearby while you
are napping; that way if you are suddenly disturbed, you can
just act like you are writing something down. Or you may
choose to kick off your shoes and prop your feet up on another
chair.

That way, not only will you be more comfortable, but if you are disturbed, you can just grab your shoe and act like you had something in it. Or you may choose to keep your shoes on while propping your feet up, so if someone bothers you, you can just be tying your shoe. It's important to remember that even if you can just close your eyes without actually falling asleep, that will still help you rest and relax.

However, if you are caught sleeping, just sign the holy cross, fold your hands and say, "amen". Say it loud enough for them to hear. That way you can just say that you were praying. If they question you on it, just say that your cousin is very ill and is in the hospital and every day you pray for him or her. That usually ends the questioning there. Another choice of a professional slacker is when you are caught just say, "Praise the almighty Allah" or "Buddha" or some ancient religious god from Egypt. If you have been caught sleeping before by the same person or boss and used the above technique already, then use it again.

Then you should follow it up by politely saying, "I'll be right with you" and immediately stand up and bow down, then kneel down and make weird sounds loudly so they get embarrassed and walk away.

If they haven't left you by now, then say, "hang on, I just got one more god to pray to" then say "ala alalala la ala la" in a high pitch voice. That way, you'll be also practicing up on your singing skills too. That should send just about anyone running.

If you are asked what religion you are, make one up. Or tell them the almighty will not allow you to discuss it. It will be harder for them to fire you because of your religious beliefs. That would be discrimination and could turn into a lawsuit that they just don't want. If you are harassed about your newly found religion, say you've been reborn again and have been practicing it for years now. If they keep bothering you, that would also be called harassment and yet another lawsuit.

So you might do a little research, on company time of course, on old ancient religions and learn a little about them; that way if a lawsuit should come up, the ball will be in your court.

So get out there and start slacking.

Note to reader: The content of this entire book has been based on actual events that have been observed over a period of years working at various jobs. All these events contained within are not my own views or practices, just the facts of observing others while they work and what happens day to day in a typical work place environment.

Glossary

Defensive Slacking – Being able to spot trouble while it is still some distance away, while always making a concerted effort to get away from the area and avoid trouble entirely.

Duck and Cover Technique – Consists of going out the opposite way of trouble and ducking into the restroom or some other safe place.

Offensive Slacking Technique – Making a co-worker or person want to avoid you by making it embarrassing or uncomfortable for them to be around you.

Procrastination Slacking – Avoiding a big task or job by concentrating on smaller, non important jobs instead, in hopes that you'll stop being asked to do big tasks or jobs.

Slackmaster – One who has mastered all the steps in slacking, knowing when, where, and how to outsmart the opponent(s), by doing the least amount of work possible.

Disclaimer:

Warning: Slacking is a form of extreme risk taking and can be habit forming. Slacking could be hazardous to your employment status. Slack at your own risk. I am in no way responsible for your actions if you shall choose to become a Slackmaster. You are responsible for your own decisions. So Proceed with caution, if you dare. The contents of these pages are for entertainment purposes only. (Maybe)

www.ingramcontent.com/pod-product-compliance
Lightning Source LLC
La Vergne TN
LVHW021515080426
835509LV00018B/2526